AD SANCTOS

AD SANCTOS

a choral performance work
bpNichol/words
Howard Gerhard/music

The Martyrology
Book 9
1986-87

Coach House Press
Toronto

Published with the assistance of the Canada Council, the Ontario Arts Council
and the Department of Communications.

The writing of *Ad Sanctos* was made possible by a grant from the Music Theatre
Development Program of the Ontario Arts Council.

Canadian Cataloguing in Publication Data

Nichol, B. P., 1944-1988
  Ad sanctos : The martyrology, book 9

ISBN 0-88910-454-9

I. Title. II. Title: The martyrology, book 9.

PS8527.I32A74 1993   C811'.54   C92-095508-8
PR9199.3.N48A74 1993

for R. Murray Schafer & John Beckwith

CONTENTS

bpNichol
preface / 9

bpNichol
Ad Sanctos: words / 13

Howard Gerhard
Ad Sanctos: music / 51

bpNichol
production notes / 299

PREFACE
bpNichol

AD SANCTOS
a music/theatre piece with Howard Gerhard

ACT I:

We hear the tail end of a play (last scene of a pageant) as a final cart loaded with actors rumbles out of the area we are watching in. There is a distant flourish of trumpets, a moment's stillness, and then a troupe of 4 or 5 rag-tag players comes rushing into the space. The leader calls on us to wait, not to leave just yet, that as a special treat they will put on a small performance for us. He explains they are poor pilgrims on their way to be buried by the tomb of their favorite saints and that they seek, thru pleasing us with their performance, to find funds for the long journey. Even as he talks more of the same group straggle onto stage until there are some twelve people assembled there. One of them now begins a small sermon on the virtue of virtue but is frequently interrupted as there is much arguing among themselves as to what constitutes virtue and a fair amount of name-calling re the shenanigans X or Y has been up to in the last few days. The narrator becomes anxious that we will become bored and tries to hold our attention with jokes, etc. and then persuades various members of the troupe to come forward and tell their story. This they do with their interjections and corrections from the other members standing around, but this way some four or five stories get told and some notion of the saints they go to be buried by. But as this information accumulates there is new consternation, the sudden realization that there are simply too many saints, that those going to the nearest ones (as it were) will reap all the benefits of the struggle but that others will be left out, end up travelling on their own thru hostile lands. A literal fight breaks out with much punching and name-calling. But out of this a compromise is arrived at; they will all travel to be buried by the tomb of the same saint. Now it remains to choose which saint, a saint they can all agree on. The list is quickly winnowed down to only one obvious choice—St. Valentine. Everyone is happy with this. The man who first spoke to us thanks us for our attention and kindness and says: "When next we meet may it be in Rome by the tomb of St. Valentine." Everyone exits through the crowd asking for donations.

ACT II:

Members of the same troupe come staggering in. The same man says to us: "Ah, we meet again. We have travelled far looking for this grave." He goes on to say they draw near their goal and different members are out looking for the appropriate grave. We hear different feelings from different members of the group about the pleasure of finally being able to rest at the foot of St. Valentine etc., more about their desires for this life and the next, the things that have drawn them on this pilgrimage. One of the people who've been searching comes rushing in from the left to say that he has found the grave. Mighty shouts & hosannas go up & the whole group begins a song of praise. As they prepare to exit towards the grave another member of the troupe comes rushing in from the right to say she has found the grave, a different grave from the first! Consternation and despair. Arguments & dissensions begin as to which is the true grave and which, therefore, the one they should die & be buried by. The group divides into three camps: one exits to the right to die & be buried by the second grave; the third, three people, remains in the middle of the stage. If the heart is divided even here, then this is a sign. There is no peace in escaping into death. The three turn and head off, back into the world.

bpNichol
draft, September 1986

some notes on the libretto. i try to write a fairly unaccented line when writing librettos (as opposed to my poetry where i work to control the cadence—and hence accent, etc.—to a high degree), the point being to allow the composer the greatest freedom of movement possible. the AD SANCTOS libretto moves back and forth between straight speech and the sung sections. the encompassing fiction of the chorus singing to raise money for their pilgrimage allows this to happen naturally. there are differences between the text of the libretto and Howie's score, differences he and i have discussed as he's gone along. there is one major change to come in the libretto i.e. the inclusion of the conductor as a character. i was hoping we could get away without a conductor but it's become obvious we can't. and i don't want the conductor to stand outside the piece. it's important that he/she be included as part of the dramatic action of the work.

bpNichol
October 1987

AD SANCTOS: WORDS
bpNichol

Setting
A public gathering place near the Flaminian Way, Rome.

Time
Unspecified.

Characters
i, carries a pitch pipe
she, a woman, carries wood blocks
he, a man, carries a penny whistle
we, carries a snare drum
they, carries cymbals
david, a man, carries a triangle
a writer, carries sticks
a reader, carries a ratchet gourd
st. agnes, a woman, carries a slide whistle
st. reat, a younger man, carries a bass drum
st. ranglehold, a man, carries a tambourine
st. orm, an older man, carries glass chimes

T he fading bars of a trumpet piece are heard, the distant shuffling of feet, and perhaps even a few last stragglers are seen to be exiting—all towards the stage left side of the playing area.

A moment passes in which nothing happens and then i, a slight figure in tattered clothing, rushes out from the stage right side of the playing area, looks out at the audience and then, looking back, shouts out:

i:

They're still here!!

i disappears again stage right. We hear a shuffling of feet, a murmur of voices, the blowing of a pitch pipe, and then i leads a rag-tag assemblage of tattered, worn, filthy human beings, all humming their beginning notes, out into the playing area. The saints have their flags raised high and each of the characters with a light is holding it up and waving it slowly back and forth. i looks out at the audience and announces unctuously:

i:

Ladies and gentlemen! For your further enjoyment some *divertissements* of a moral nature to incite the virtue of charity in your hearts.

i takes off a hat i has been wearing and holds it out as if asking for money, and then turns the gesture into a small bow and announces the title:

i:

"A Singer's Hell: An Instruction on the Nature of Sanctity and Scarcity."

The singers, who have been humming &/or singing their tones all along, now begin.

i:

So shall

she:

the world

he:

go on,

we:

To good

they:

malignant,

david:

to bad

a writer:

men

a reader:

benign,

st. reat:

Under

st. agnes:

her own

st. ranglehold:

weight

st. orm:

groaning

The singers' faces are wreathed in anguish as they sing. They begin to writhe like tableaus from Doré's engravings of Milton's visions of Hell. As this piece unfolds, i conducts it as well as singing a part, occasionally casting anxious looks back at the audience. i's anxiety is heightened each time i looks back; i's becoming convinced the piece is bombing complete-ly. Finally i steps towards the front of the playing area and looking out asks:

i:

Is all this clear? We've been accused of a bit of obscurity in
some of the towns we've passed thru and ...

i's voice trails away. i looks back at the singers and then, going back, begins to
whisper in their ears, one by one, suggesting a change to something lighter,
something sprightlier. And one by one they begin to shift into a totally different
mood and temperament.

chorus:

we are going to   saints
we are going to   saints
we are going to   saints

      we are going to   saints
      we are going to   saints
      we are going to   saints

sacred saints   fabulous & faithful
saints of language saints of spirit saints
of song of being blessed

we are going to   saints
we are going to   saints
we are going to   saints

      we are going to   saints
      we are going to   saints
      we are going to   saints

sacred saints (saints)   fabulous & faithful
saints (saints) of language saints (saints)
of spirit saints (saints) of song of being blessed
yes yes yes yes yes yes yes yes yes yes yes yes

we are going to   saints
we are going to   saints
we are going to   saints

      we are going to   saints
      we are going to   saints
      we are going to   saints

sacred saints   fabulous & faithful
saints of language saints of spirit saints
of song of being blessed

we are going to   saints
we are going to   saints
we are going to   saints

        we are going to   saints
        we are going to   saints
        we are going to   saints

sacred saints (saints)   fabulous & faithful
saints (saints) of language saints (saints)
of spirit saints (saints) of song of being blessed
yes yes yes yes yes yes yes yes yes yes yes yes
saints saints saints saints saints saints saints saints

chorus: **chorus:**

saints		saints
saints	**they:**	saints
saints		saints
saints	what is that which is	saints
saints	what is that which was	saints
saints	what is that which will be	saints
saints	blessed	saints
saints		saints
saints	who is that which is	saints
saints	who is that which was	saints
saints	who is that which will be	saints
saints	sainted	saints
saints		saints
saints	where is that which is	saints
saints	where is that which was	saints
saints	where it that which will be	saints
saints	translated	saints
saints		saints
saints	why is that which is	saints
saints	why is that which was	saints
saints	why is that which will be	saints
saints	divine	saints
saints		saints

```
saints                  he:                 saints
saints                                      saints
saints          signs                       saints
saints          give me signs               saints
saints                                      saints
saints              they & he:              saints
saints                                      saints
saints          give us signs               saints
saints                                      saints
saints            they, he & she:           saints
saints                                      saints
saints          give us signs      give us signs   saints
saints                                      saints
saints          they, he, she & we:         saints
saints                                      saints
saints          give us signs signs signs   saints
saints                                      saints
saints give us signs give us signs give us signs saints
give us signs give us signs give us signs give us signs give us signs
give us signs give us signs give us signs give us signs give us signs
give us signs give us signs give us signs give us signs give us signs
give us signs give us signs give us signs give us signs give us signs
give us a sign give us a sign give us a sign give us a sign give us a
  sign give us a sign give us a sign give us a sign give us a sign give
us a sign give us a sign give us a sign give us a sign give us a sign
  give us a sign give us a sign give us a sign give us a sign give us a
sign
```

As the **chorus** continues, becoming softer and softer, i steps forward and addresses the audience.

i:

You can see the problem. Even belief takes money. Otherwise your belief in belief fades. But how do you ask for it without seeming ... hypocritical? So ...

(**i** gestures at the **chorus**)

... we try to offer a little entertainment, a little instruction, in return for your hard-earned coin. We share the same difficulty after all.

a reader:
(shouts from the **chorus**)

Tell 'em where we're going.

i:
(flustered)

Ah ... yes. We're off to visit the tomb of St. Valentine. To spend our days in praise and to die and be buried next to him.

david:

A holy pilgrimage.

i removes i's hat again, and places it at the very front of the playing area.

i:

And of course we need your assistance.

There is little or no response from the audience.

i:
(looking around sadly)

We have been on the road a long time now.

he:
(shouting from the **chorus**)

Let's give 'em something more familiar.

i:

More familiar? Well ...

he:

Sure! Give 'em Saint Reat's song.

st. reat:

That old chestnut!!

i:

Alright! Alright! No schisms. We're trying to raise a little money here. (blows on his pitch pipe) Ready?

he, she, we, they, david, a writer & a reader:

Oh let me sing
Oh let me dance
Oh God please give me
A second chance

I was never for prayer
I was never for peace
I was never that happy
I was never that pleased

But oh let me sing
Oh let me dance
Oh God please give me
A second chance

As the seven members of the **chorus** sing the above, the four saints attempt an awkward little dance. In the middle of it, **st. reat** and **st. orm** take a wrong turn and crash into each other, knocking each other to the floor. The seven-member **chorus** sings on behind them.

st. orm:
(stage whisper)

You fool! Watch what you're doing!!

st. reat:
(stage whisper)

If you'd keep those bananas you call feet peeled, this wouldn't have happened.

i:
(dragging them both to their feet)

SHHH!!
(casts despairing glance at audience)
Keep dancing!

They continue their awkward dance. As the piece ends a member of the audience walks to the front and puts some money in the hat and then returns and sits down again. **i** is beside himself with gratitude.

i:

Oh thank you! Thank you!!

i pauses, looking around expectantly at the rest of the audience. After whatever response i gets:

i:

Would it help to hear something of each pilgrim's life? We are a troupe, a community really. And we have forsaken the selfishness of the individual or ...
                    (throws a glance at the saints)
... at least we've tried to.

st. orm:

Fat lot of good it's done us.

i ignores him, looks around at the audience for a moment, and then, shrugging, blows the opening note on the pitch pipe:

chorus:

a life
a life
a life
a life
a life
a life
a life
a life
a life
a life   **st. reat:**
a life
a life   Was i not a saint?
a life   What of it?
a life   All that in another time.
a life   Is not a saint but
a life   one who dies?
a life   Are not our lives but
a life   endless questions
a life   noone answers?
a life   No noone answers.

a life   We rush on
a life   towards our death
a life   & sainted
a life   leave this life.
a life
a life
a life
a life
a life   **david:**
a life
a life   My life is made of many
a life   lives & lines all intersecting,
a life   many deaths in
a life   all these lifetimes.
a life   Each one treasured
a life   as special, unique,
a life   grieved over when departed
a life   by those, too, who are departed
a life   so long ago there is none now to grieve.
a life   Me—we too
a life   in time, these many lives
a life   all passed, all forgotten,
a life   no longer special, no longer
a life   unique, no longer
a life   grieved over. Over. Simply over.
a life   The many over & the many done &
a life   the many gone who thought of themselves as
a life   one.
a life
a life
a life
a life
a life
a life   **a reader:**
a life
a life   And of *my* life, who cares?
a life   as long as i was there to do as bidden.
a life   i have lived out my life in service
a life   to one pre-set path after another,
a life   brought each one to a conclusion & never thanked.
a life   not once. patronized rather. matronized.
a life   treated as interchangeable
a life   with all the others like me.
a life   my death unremarked. my place

a life	taken by another. all the same.
a life	all the same.
a life	
a life	
a life	
a life	
a life	
a life	**a writer:**
a life	
a life	And i have withheld details, confused
a life	by this business of a story
a life	a life story. ah but i have rushed on &
a life	told so many, &
a life	still the clamour for more, details.
a life	details. who had thought to embrace death
a life	& deny immortality as a saint.
a life	as a saint would, dying.
a life	and they give you then a name.
a life	a stone. saint. st. one.
a life	
a life	
a life	
a life	
a life	
a life	**we:**
a life	
a life	Was i not a saint?
a life	lives & lines all intersecting
a life	i have lived out my life in service
a life	told so many, all there, &
a life	one who dies?
a life	as special, unique,
a life	treated as interchangeable
a life	as a saint would, dying.
a life	No noone answers.
a life	Me—we too
a life	all the same.
a life	
a life	
a life	
a life	
a life	all i've
a life	all i've
a life	all i've alive

a life	all i've	alive	
a life	all i've	alive	
a life	all i've	alive	a death
a life	all i've	alive	a death
a life	all i've	alive	a death
a life	all i've	alive	a death
a life			a death
a life			a death
a life			a death
a life			a death
a life			a death
a life			a death
a life			a death
a life			a death
a life			a death
a life			a death
a life			a death
a life			a death

During all of the preceding, i keeps a wary eye on the audience. Now, as the voices fade, i steps forward again; gesturing at the hat which is still sitting on the very front of the playing area.

i:

lives. our lives. a saint's life. & now to dedicate this life to praising a saint that we may join him in that life ...

There is a sudden disruption in the **chorus. st. reat** & **st. orm** are pushing & shoving at each other. **st. ranglehold** & **st. agnes** are trying to separate them.

st. reat:

don't give me any of your holier-than-thou talk! i've suffered too.

st. orm:

suffered?! you don't even know the meaning of the word "suffer"!

st. agnes:

c'mon you two! break it up. i'm sick of listening to you argue.
(aside to **a writer**)

there's nothing worse than two old fools, who think they're holy men, arguing.

i rushes back to assist in separating them as **st. orm** takes a swing at **st. reat** & hits **st. ranglehold** instead. **st. ranglehold** drops, moaning.

i:

gentle sirs! gentlefolk! this is an entertainment, not a brawl! not a time for settling old antagonisms.

a reader throws up his hands in despair.

a reader:

i told you there was no point in this pilgrimage. we'll never succeed.
(then turning to a writer)
you get a feeling for these things after awhile. you can tell by the way it begins how the whole thing's going to end.

we:

unity! unity!

a desperate **we** pulls out a pitch pipe &, blowing it to sound the starting pitch, begins to conduct everyone except **i** & the saints in the singing of a praise-song on the theme of unity. all thru this **st. orm** keeps taking swings at **st. reat** and **st. reat** swings back. they curse each other and flail ineffectually.

chorus (sung):	**st. reat** (spoken):
oh that in this life we	you're nothing but a has been!
strive together to be	
united peacefully	**st. orm:**
through wars & famine	
plague & the earth's own toll	an am.
to be we to be we to be we	
when all about us people die	**st. reat:**
& when they die they die alone	
under the sword or	a was.
the earth's harsh groan	
and heave. yet to be we	**st. orm:**
to be we to be we	
strive together peacefully	an is.

to be we   to be we   to be we   **st. reat:**
to be we   to be we   to be we

                 a shouldn't have been.

                    st. orm:

                 and shall be again.

As the **chorus** finishes, the two saints slump back exhaustedly.

                   i:
             (pointing at the saints)

they were all saints themselves you know.
gave it up. all that "me me me" of
sainthood. the idea was to merge
ourselves into a larger body, to forget
ourselves by praising another.
                 (he shrugs)
and look at this!
                 (gestures at the saints again)
it took so long to draw us together. to
agree on a saint we could spend our days
praising.
                 (looks up beseechingly)
and did you not give us those signs,
Valentine?

At which point the **chorus** begins to sing the following:

                 she:

       did not my heart break   valentine?
            was that a sign?

                            he:

                 did not my heart ache   valentine?
                     was that a sign?

            they:

     did not my heart freeze   valentine?
            was that a sign?

we:

did not my heart ease   valentine?
was that a sign?

david:

did not my heart need   valentine?
was that a sign?

i:

did not my heart bleed   valentine?
was that a sign?

a reader:

did not my heart yearn   valentine?
was that a sign?

a writer:

did not my heart burn   valentine?
was that a sign?

st. agnes:

did not my heart seek   valentine?
was that a sign?

st. reat:

did not my heart speak   valentine?
was that a sign?

st. ranglehold:

did not my heart sigh   valentine?
was that a sign?

st. orm:

did not my heart cry   valentine?
was that a sign?

chorus:

sign   design   signal   sign
design   signal   sign   design
signal   sign   design   signal
sign   design   signal   sign
design   signal   sign   design
signal   sign   design   signal
sign   design   signal   sign
design   signal   sign   design
signal   sign   design   signal
sign   design   signal   sign
design   signal   sign   design
signal   sign   design   signal
sign   design   signal   sign
design   signal   sign   design
signal   sign   design   signal
sign   design   signal   sign
design   signal   sign   design
signal   sign   design   signal
sign   design   signal   sign
design   signal   sign   design
signal   sign   design   signal
sign   design   signal   sign
design   signal   sign   design
signal   sign   design   signal
sign   design   signal   sign
design   signal   sign   design
signal   sign   design   signal
sign   design   signal   sign
design   signal   sign   design
signal   sign   design   signal
sign   design   signal   sign
design   signal   sign   design
signal   sign   design   signal
sign   design   signal   sign
design   signal   sign   design
signal   sign   design   signal

st. orm:

sign of my faith
in you.

a writer:

sign of my love
in you.

st. agnes:

sign of belief
in you.

a reader:

sign of my hope
in you.

st. ranglehold:

sign of my path
in you.

they:

sign of my way
in you.

st. reat:

sign of my song

(As this
is being
sung, the
chorus
uses a
number of
ways to
sign the
word
"sign."
The
saints
use
semaphore
flags
(see
NOTES at
end). **we,
she, he &
they** use
deaf sign
language.
The re-
maining
four use
lights to
morse
code the
word.)

```
sign   design      signal    sign      in you.
design      signal    sign   design
   signal    sign   design      signal
sign   design      signal    sign          we:
design      signal    sign   design
   signal    sign   design      signal    sign of my prayer
sign   design      signal    sign      in you.
design      signal    sign   design
   signal    sign   design      signal
sign   design      signal    sign
design      signal    sign   design         david:
   signal    sign   design      signal
sign   design      signal    sign      sign of my life
design      signal    sign   design      in you.
   signal    sign   design      signal
sign   design      signal    sign
design      signal    sign   design          she:
   signal    sign   design      signal
sign   design      signal    sign      sign of my death
design      signal    sign   design      in you.
   signal    sign   design      signal
sign   design      signal    sign
design      signal    sign   design           he:
   signal    sign   design      signal
sign   design      signal    sign      sign of my sign
design      signal    sign   design      in you.
   signal    sign   design      signal
sign   design      signal    sign
design      signal    sign   design            i:
   signal    sign   design      signal
sign   design      signal    sign      sign of my time
design      signal    sign   design      in you.
   signal    sign   design      signal
sign   design      signal    sign
design      signal    sign   design
   signal    sign   design      signal
```

time
t-time
t-t-time
t-t-t-time
t-t-t-t-time
t-t-t-t-t-time
t-t-t-t-t-t-time
t-t-t-t-t-t-t-time
t-t-t-t-t-t-t-t-time
t-t-t-t-t-t-t-t-t-time
t-t-t-t-t-t-t-t-t-t-time
t-t-t-t-t-t-t-t-t-t-t-time
t-t-t-t-t-t-t-t-t-t-t-t-time
t-t-t-t-t-t-t-t-t-t-t-t-t-time
t-t-t-t-t-t-t-t-t-t-t-t-t-t-time
t-t-t-t-t-t-t-t-t-t-t-t-t-t-t-time
t-t-t-t-t-t-t-t-t-t-t-t-t-t-t-t-time
t-t-t-t-t-t-t-t-t-t-t-t-t-t-t-t-t-time
t-t-t-t-t-t-t-t-t-t-t-t-t-t-t-t-t-t-time
t-t-t-t-t-t-t-t-t-t-t-t-t-t-t-t-t-t-t-time
t-t-t-t-t-t-t-t-t-t-t-t-t-t-t-t-t-t-t-t-time
t-t-t-t-t-t-t-t-t-t-t-t-t-t-t-t-t-t-t-t-t-time
t-t-t-t-t-t-t-t-t-t-t-t-t-t-t-t-t-t-t-t-t-t-time
t-t-t-t-t-t-t-t-t-t-t-t-t-t-t-t-t-t-t-t-t-t-t-time
t-time t-time t-time t-time t-time t-time t-time
t-t-t-t-t-t-t-t-t-t-t-t-t-t-t-t-t-t-t-t-t-t-t-t-t-t-t-
t-t-t-t-t-t-t-t-t-t-t-t-t-t-t-t-t-t-t-t-t-t-t-t-t-t-t-
t-t-t-t-t-t-t-t-t-t-t-t-t-t-t-t-t-t-t-t-t-t-t-t-t-t-t-

(As the **chorus** moves into this section they all raise their arms & begin to move them like clock hands, an hour at a time. Each "clock" is free to begin at whatever time it chooses. Movements should be loosely coordinated but need not be exact (like the clocks one sees on display in clock shops))

st. orm:	a writer:	st. agnes:	a reader:	st. ranglehold:	they:
t		b		g	
t		b		g	
t		b		g	
t		b		g	
t		b		g	
t		b		g	
t		b		g	
t	d	b	k	g	p
t	d	b	k	g	p
t	d	b	k	g	p
t	d	b	k	g	p
t	d	b	k	g	p
t	d	b	k	g	p
t	d	b	k	g	p
t	d	b	k	g	p
	d		k		p

st. reat:		david:		he:	
	d		k		p
	d		k		p
t	d	b	k	g	p
t	d	b	k	g	p
t	d	b	k	g	p
t	d	b	k	g	p
t		b		g	

	we:		she:		i:
t		b		g	
t		b		g	
t	d	b	k	g	p
t	d	b	k	g	p
t	d	b	k	g	p
t	d	b	k	g	p
t	d	b	k	g	p
t	d	b	k	g	p
t	d	b	k	g	p
t	d	b	k	g	p
t	d	b	k	g	p
	d		k		p
	d		k		p
	d		k		p
	d		k		p
	d		k		p
	d		k		p
	d		k		p

chorus:
(gradually slowing down)

t t t t t t t t t t t t t t t t t t t t t t t t t t t t t t t t

As the **chorus** winds down, they continue to move their arms. There are thirty seconds of complete silence during which the tempo of their arm movements increases & becomes more pronouncedly jerky. Suddenly they all stop at once. i takes a tentative step forward.

i:

and so we go to seek St. Valentine's grave that we might praise him.

At this point **she** exits to the left & **he** exits to the right. i turns to watch them go & then turns back to the audience.

i:

we are close now. but there is the problem of money. faith costs money. only a little, but a little nonetheless.
        (i gestures after the departed players)
they have gone to seek St. Valentine's grave. their path is clear. ours is not clear
        (i points to the almost empty hat)
that hat. that same same hat.
(i bends over, picks it up, removes the money then places the hat on i's head)
you can beg, but i was taught not to. give value for value my parents always said. and i can't prove what God will give you if you give to me. how can i know, really.
        (i looks around then leans forward, confidentially)
do you believe i'm divinely inspired?
        (i pauses, then laughs)
well somebody dictated this speech to me.

Now **st. orm** yells at him from the **chorus** who have been standing casually behind him.

st. orm:

c'mon! more entertainment. less preaching.

st. agnes:

we gave all that up when we gave up our own sainthood.

they:
(to **st. orm**)

what's wrong with preaching? we just sang them a love song.

we:

so sing them another one.

st. ranglehold:

something sweet.

david:

familiar.

i:
(to the **chorus,** announcing the title)

"This Is A Love Song."

chorus nods, pleased. everyone hums their pitch.

chorus:

this is a love song

        this is a love song

wrote it on the long road   singing

        wrote it on the long road   singing

nearly home

        nearly home

a

b

c   **david:**

d   city of love, i have imagined,
city of peace, your squares &

e   dwellings, devoid of palaces &
citadels, houses of power & of war,

f   not banished but never desired. city
i've wandered dreaming, have dwelt in &

g   called home.

h

                                                half-chorus:

i

                             this is a love song

j

                             wrote it on the long road   singing

k

                             nearly home

l

m

n

o   **st. agnes:**

p   home, or a heaven, a haven or
simply being. here. in the world.

q   this world &
therefore i praise. therefore i sing of

r   the heart. celebrate the dwelling place.
that which is. that which is.

s   that which is.

t

                                                  half-chorus:

u

                             this is a love song

v

                             wrote it on the long road   singing

w

                             nearly home

x

y

z   **chorus:**

this is a love song

wrote it on the long road   singing

nearly home

this is a love song

this is a love song

                                          singing

                                          singing

nearly home

this is a love song

this is a love song

                                          singing

                                          singing

nearly home
nearly home
nearly home
nearly home
nearly home
nearly home
nearly home
nearly home
nearly home
nearly home
nearly home
nearly home
nearly home
nearly home
nearly home
nearly home

nearly home
nearly home
nearly home
nearly home
nearly home
nearly home
nearly home
nearly home
nearly home
nearly home
nearly home
nearly home
nearly home
nearly home
nearly home
nearly home
nearly home
nearly home
nearly home
nearly home
nearly home
nearly home
nearly home
nearly home
nearly home
nearly home
nearly home
nearly home
nearly home
nearly home
nearly home
nearly home
nearly home
nearly home
nearly home

Even as the **chorus** is ending this song, **she** comes rushing in from the left.

she:

i've found it! i've found the tomb of St. Valentine!!

A spontaneous cheer goes up.

i:

are you sure?

she:

of course i'm sure. it's got his name on it.

i falls to i's knees, arms raised, gazing up at the heavens.

i:

bless us father mother. bless you. bless St. Valentine ...

st. orm:

enough blessings! let's get going. when we're this close why
hang around here?

The mood's been broken for **i**. i stands up, brushing the dirt off the knees of i's
trousers.

i:

no need to be rude. i was just taking a moment out to praise.

st. orm:

we've been doing nothing but praising for the last half hour.
we'll all be dead before we reach the tomb.

And **st. orm** stalks off towards the left. he pauses just before exiting & looks back.

st. orm:

well?

i:

i still think a blessing, a song of praise, is in order.

st. orm:
(sneering)

order?!
(looks around)
what do any of you know of order?

& **st. orm** turns & leaves. there is a moment of uncomfortable silence & then **i** blows the pitch pipe once again.

i:

don't let him destroy the spirituality of the moment. together now.

chorus:

bless bless bless bless sing
bless bless bless bless sing
bless bless bless bless sing
sing bless sing bless sing
sing bless sing bless sing
sing bless sing bless sing
bless bless bless bless sing
bless bless bless bless sing
bless bless bless bless sing
sing bless sing bless sing
sing bless sing bless sing
sing bless sing bless sing
bless bless bless bless sing
bless bless bless bless sing
bless bless bless bless sing
sing bless sing bless sing
sing bless sing bless sing
sing bless sing bless sing
bless bless bless bless sing
bless bless bless bless sing
bless bless bless bless sing
sing bless sing bless sing
sing bless sing bless sing
sing bless sing bless sing
bless bless bless bless sing
bless bless bless bless sing
bless bless bless bless sing
sing bless sing bless sing
sing bless sing bless sing
sing bless sing bless sing
bless bless bless bless sing

david:

bless you. less me when i
bless you. more me con a-
more, blessing you.

she:

bless you. less me when i
bless you. more me con a-
more, blessing you.

they:

bless you. less us when we
bless you. more we con a-
more, blessing you.

david & she:

bless you. less me when i
bless you. more we con a-

```
bless bless bless bless sing                    more, blessing you.
bless bless bless bless sing
sing  bless sing  bless sing
sing  bless sing  bless sing
sing  bless sing  bless sing
bless bless bless bless sing
bless bless bless bless sing
bless bless bless bless sing
sing  bless sing  bless sing
sing  bless sing  bless sing          david, she & they:
sing  bless sing  bless sing
bless bless bless bless sing          bless you. less us when we
bless bless bless bless sing          bless you. more we con a-
bless bless bless bless sing          more, blessing you.
sing  bless sing  bless sing
sing  bless sing  bless sing
sing  bless sing  bless sing
bless bless bless bless sing
bless bless bless bless sing  you
bless bless bless bless sing  you
sing  bless sing  bless sing  you
sing  bless sing  bless sing  you
sing  bless sing  bless sing  you
                bless sing  you
           sing  you  bless sing  you
                      bless sing  you
                 sing  you  bless sing  you
                           bless sing  you
```

As they sing the closing part of the song, the **chorus** begins to troop off to the left following the already departed **st. orm**. just as the first person goes to exit, **he** rushes in from the right.

he:

i've found it! i've found the tomb of St. Valentine!

Everyone stops abruptly with much bumping into each other, cursing and consternation.

i:

what?

st. reat:

how can that be?

a writer:

are you sure?

They all turn and stare angrily at **he**.

he:
(taken aback)

sure? of course i'm sure. it's got his name on it

he points back the way **he**'s just come from.

he:

come & see.

a reader:

we were just going.

he:

home?

st. agnes:

we thought so.

he:

giving up?

st. ranglehold:

no. going.

they:

to the tomb.

he:

the one i found.

she:

the one i found.

he:

you found? but that's impossible.

david:

a miracle?

i:

impossible.

she:

i found the tomb of St. Valentine.

he:

i found the tomb of St. Valentine.

she & he:

They glare at each other for a moment.

she:

there is only one true tomb and therefore only one real way to choose.

he:

exactly.

you've done this to discredit me, haven't you?

why would i bother? you discredit yourself.

Everyone else is following this argument, torn back and forth by prior loyalties, commitments to ideals, etc. At this point **he** & **she** withdraw to opposite sides of the stage. **she** begins to sing:

she:

No path but the true path
should be taken.

he:

No road but the holy road,
the way.

she:

All other roads are
mistaken.

he:

When the true path is
taken, the way is clear,

she & he:

tho the true path be not the near path
& the price be dear,
no path but the true path
should be taken. No road but
the holy road, the way. All other roads
are mistaken.

Now everyone joins in. This is sung as a combination of a series of monologues and conversations.

No path but the true path
should be taken. No road but the
holy road, the way. All other roads are
mistaken. When the true path is
taken, the way is clear, tho
the true path be not the near path
& the price be dear,
no path but the true path
should be taken. No road but
the holy road, the way. All other roads are
mistaken & when taken
lead to loneliness, lovelessness,
lead to emptiness, bitterness,
lead to nothingness, lead away.

the words in the last three lines ("loneliness," "lovelessness," "emptiness," "bitterness" & "nothingness") are picked up and sung by various members of the **chorus** as solo lines and then **i** sings the last line of the song:

i:

away.

she & **he** are still standing on opposite sides of the playing area glaring at each other.

she:

i know what i saw.

he:

and i.

she:

anyone who wishes to follow me to the true tomb is welcome.

he:

i extend the same invitation.

The rest of the **chorus** look back & forth between **she** & **he**, & then at each other.

a writer:

her speech has the ring of truth to it.

a reader:

i was about to say the same about his.

a writer:

i think i'll follow her.

a reader:

him.

And they walk to join their chosen side. The rest of the **chorus** looks around & then with shrugs or sneers moves to one or the other side of the playing area.

we:

how can we know the true tomb when there are two.

they:

we know the messengers. we know who we can trust.

we & **david** join **she** & **a writer** on the left; **they** & **st. reat** join **he** & **a reader** on the right; **i, st. agnes** & **st. ranglehold** move towards the front centre of the playing area.

she & the others exit to the left; **he** & the others exit to the right; **i, st. agnes** & **st. ranglehold** are left alone in the playing area. **i** sits down dejectedly.

i:

and we seemed so close.

st. agnes:
(shrugging)

it's always this way.

                              i:
                        (looking up)

it is?

                        st. ranglehold:

the same ones who make you saints take your sainthood away.

                          st. agnes:

it's the nature of it.

                        st. ranglehold:

a lesson in the imperfectibility of perfection.

                              i:
                      (looking down again)
but we were so close.

st. agnes & **st. ranglehold** reach down and, each taking an arm, lift **i** up.

                          st. agnes:

i've come to believe that's the point.

                        st. ranglehold:

when you come right down to it ... if there are two valentines ...

                          st. agnes:

... two hearts ...

                        st. ranglehold:

if even here there is, after all, such a division ...
                          (he shrugs)
one and one makes one zero.

                              i:

what?

st. agnes:

the heart's a binary system. one and one makes one zero.

And then the three of them together begin to sing.

i, st. agnes & st. ranglehold:

one and one makes one zero
one and one makes one zero
one and one makes one zero
one and one makes one zero
one and one makes one zero
one and one makes one zero
one and one makes one zero
one and one makes one zero
one and one makes one zero
one and one makes one zero
one and one makes one zero
one and one makes one zero
one and one makes one zero
one and one makes one zero
one and one makes one zero
one and one makes one zero

As they sing they begin to move forward out of the playing area and exit through the audience. We still hear them singing. Tho they are no longer in sight we hear their singing end just as **st. orm** comes striding out onto the playing area and then, hearing them, follows them out through the audience.

st. orm:
(under his breath)

bloody fools!

AD SANCTOS: MUSIC
Howard Gerhard

so shall the world go on...

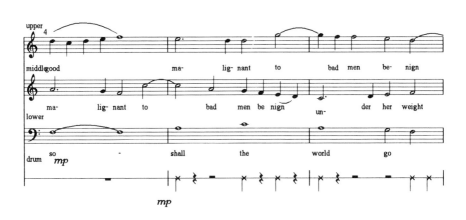

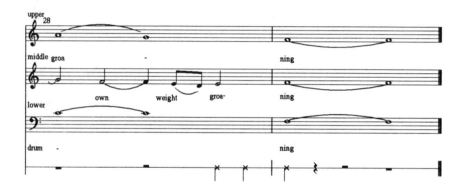

we're going to saints

loudly

(cont.)

she

we

saints go'ng to

mf

we're go ing to saints we're go ing to saints we're go ing to saints

david

st orm

chorus

chorus

violin 1

violin 2

flutes

bass

perc

mf

perc

you

we are going we are going

softly

(cont.)

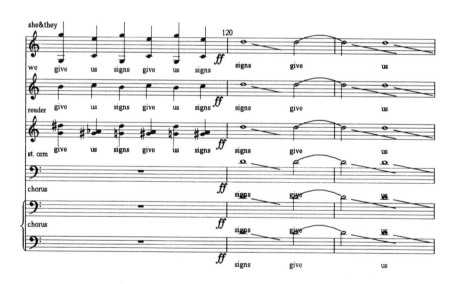

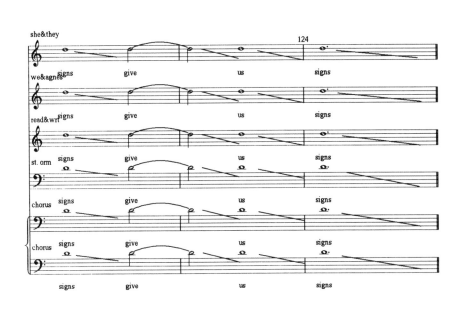

o let me sing

a life

we

a reader

st. reat

all that in a-no- ther time   is

st. orm

chorus   life   life   a life   life   life   life   a

chorus

of it   what of it   what of it   what of it

perc

bell

you

we

a reader

24

st. reat

life   is made of ma- ny lives   and lives   all in- ter- sec-ting   ma- ny deaths so ma- ny deaths   in

st. orm

life   life   life   life   a life   life

chorus

chorus

noone an-swers   no   ---

perc

bell

you

we

a reader

36

st. reat

st. orm

we too intime these ma-ny lives all

chorus life life a life life a life a life a life a life a life a life a life a life a

chorus a

life a life so longa- go a

perc

an- swers no an- swers a life a life so longa- go a

bell

you

we

a reader

there   to   do   as   bid- den   i've   lived   my   life   in

st. reat

st. orm

chorus

i've   all i've   all i've   all

chorus

cares who cares who cares who cares who cares   sim-   ply

perc

bell

you

we

a reader
ser- vice to one pre- set path af ter a- no- ther

st. reat

st. orm
i've all i've all i've

chorus

chorus
o- ver sim- ply o- ver

perc

bell

you

we

84

a reader

all the same all the same all the same all the same all the same all the same

st. reat

con- fused by this bus'- ness of a

st. orm

all the same all the same all the same all the same all the same all the same

chorus

chorus

all the same all the same all the same all the same all the same all the same

perc

bell

you

we

a reader   same   all   the   same   all   the   same   all   the   same   all   the   same   all   the   same   all   the

st. reat   all   the   same   all   the   same   all   the   same   all   the   same   all   the   same   all   the   same

st. orm   de-   ny   im-   mor-   ta-   li-   ty   as   a

chorus

chorus

perc

bell

you

that in this life

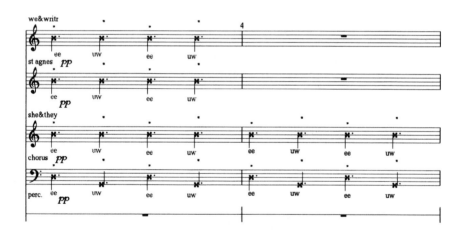

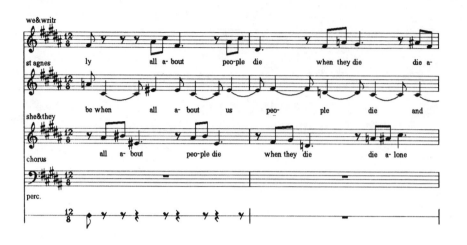

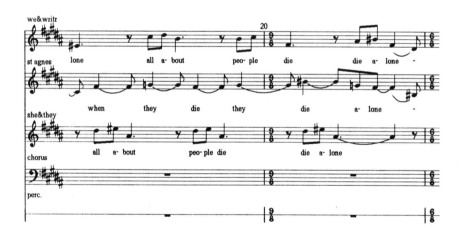

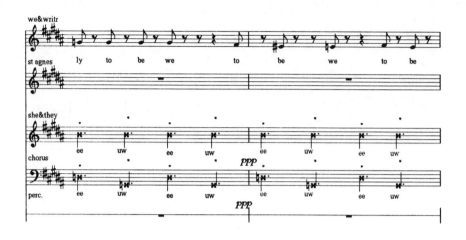

was that a sign

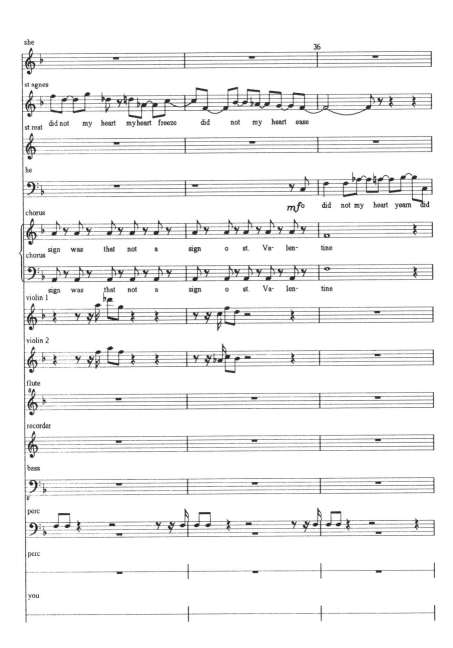

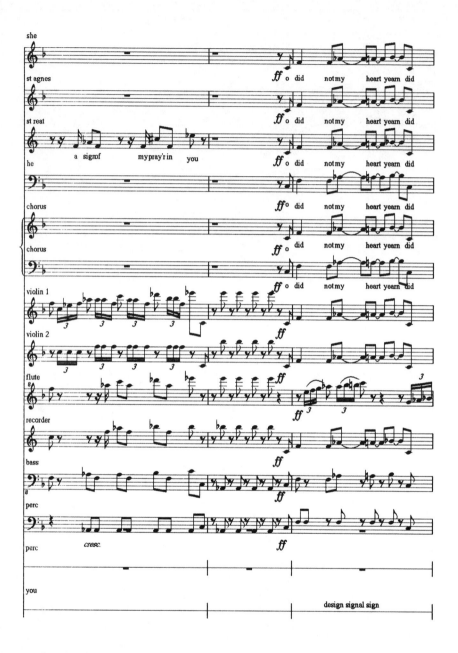

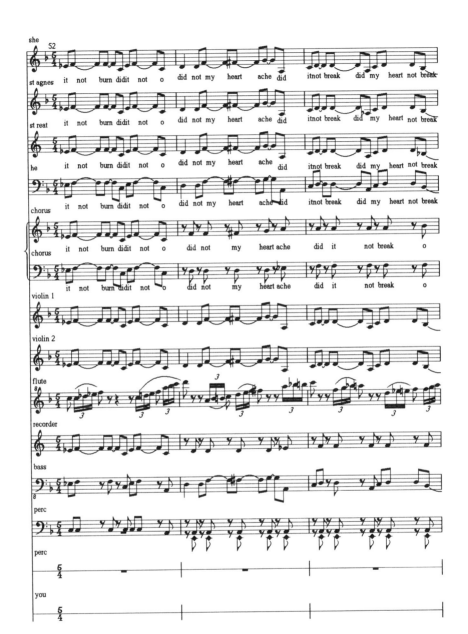

this is a love song

abcdefghijklmnopqrstuvwxyz...

slow, continuous recitation

st agnes

david

chorus

chorus

violin 1

violin 2

cello

bass

perc

you

st agnes

12

david

chorus

chorus

violin 1

violin 2

cello

bass

perc

you

st agnes

st agnes

david

chorus

chorus

violin 1

violin 2

cello

bass

perc

you

st agnes

24

david

chorus

chorus

violin 1

violin 2

cello

bass

perc

you

st agnes

david

chorus

chorus

this

violin 1

violin 2

cello

bass

perc

you

st agnes

st agnes

36

david

chorus

chorus   on   the   long   road   sin-   ging   near-   ly

violin 1

violin 2

cello

bass

perc

you

st agnes

40

david

chorus

chorus   home

violin 1

violin 2

cello

bass

perc

you

st agnes

44

david

chorus

chorus

this is a love   song   wrote it on the

violin 1

violin 2

cello

bass

perc

you

st agnes

david

chorus

chorus

road   this   is   a   love   song   a   love   song   this

violin 1

violin 2

cello

bass

perc

you

48

david

chorus

chorus

is a   love   song   wrote it on the long   road   near - - ly

violin 1

violin 2

cello

bass

perc

you

st agnes

56

david

chorus

chorus

violin 1   home

violin 2

cello

bass

perc

f   *cresc.*   *f*

you

st agnes

60

st agnes

64

david

chorus

chorus

violin 1

violin 2

mf

cello

bass

perc

you

st agnes

68

david

ci- ty of love   i   have   i-

chorus

chorus

violin 1

violin 2

cello

bass

perc

you

st agnes

72

st agnes

80

david

chorus   ba- nished   but   ne- ver de- sired   ci-   ty   i've   wan- dered   drea- ming

chorus

chorus

violin 1

violin 2

cello

bass

perc

you

st agnes

david

havedwelt in   and called   home

chorus

chorus

violin 1

violin 2

cello

bass

perc

you

st agnes

88

david

chorus

chorus

violin 1

violin 2

cello

bass

perc

you

st agnes

92

david

chorus

chorus

violin 1

violin 2

cello

bass

perc

you

96

david

chorus

this   is   a   love   song   near-   ly home

chorus

violin 1

violin 2

cello

bass

perc

you

this   is   a love   song   near-   ly   home

st agnes

david

chorus

chorus

violin 1

violin 2

cello

bass

perc

you

st agnes

david

chorus

chorus   this   is   a   love   song   wrote   it

violin 1

violin 2

cello

bass

perc

you

st agnes

david

chorus

chorus

on   the   long   road   near-   ly

violin 1

violin 2

cello

bass

perc

you

st agnes

david

chorus

chorus

violin 1

violin 2

cello

bass

perc

you

120

st agnes

david

chorus

chorus

violin 1

violin 2

cello

bass

perc

you

st agnes

128

st agnes

david here in the world this world and there-fore i praise there-fore i sing of the

chorus

chorus

violin 1

violin 2

cello

bass

perc

you

st agnes

140

heart ce-le-brate the dwel-ling place that which is that which is

david

chorus

chorus

p near- ly home

violin 1

violin 2

cello

bass

perc

you

st agnes

that which is

david

chorus

chorus   near-   ly home   near-   ly home

violin 1

violin 2

cello

bass

perc

you

st agnes

148

david

chorus

chorus

near- ly home near- ly home

violin 1

violin 2

cello

mp

bass

perc

you

st agnes

152

st agnes

david

chorus

chorus

near- ly home sin- ging

violin 1

violin 2

cello

bass

perc

you

st agnes

156

david

chorus

chorus

violin 1

violin 2

cello

bass

perc

you

st agnes

160

david

chorus

chorus

violin 1

violin 2

cello

bass

perc

you

david

chorus

chorus

violin 1 this is a love

violin 2

cello

bass

perc

you

david

chorus

chorus

violin 1   song   this   is   a   love   song

violin 2

cello

bass

perc

you

st agnes

172

st agnes

david

chorus

chorus

violin 1   home   this   is   a   love   song

violin 2

cello

bass

perc

you

st agnes

184

st agnes

188

david

chorus

is   a   love   song   this   is   a   love   song

chorus

violin 1

violin 2

cello

bass

perc

you

st agnes

192

david

chorus

wrote   it   on   the   long   road

chorus

violin 1

violin 2

cello

bass

perc

you

st agnes

david

chorus

near-   ly   home   near-   -   ly

chorus

violin 1

violin 2

cello

bass

perc

you

st agnes

david

chorus

home

chorus

violin 1

violin 2

cello

bass

perc

you

st agnes

david

chorus

chorus

violin 1

violin 2

cello

bass

perc

you

st agnes

david

chorus

chorus

violin 1

violin 2

cello

bass

perc

you

st agnes

212

st agnes

david

chorus

chorus

violin 1

violin 2

cello

bass

perc

you

BlesSing

very sssssoftly

she

a reader you less me when i bless you bless me

we   *mf*

st agnes   bless bless sing

david   *mp* bless bless sing

st reat   *mp* bless bless sing

st orm   bless bless sing

strangle

you

blessss   me   blessss   you   blesssing

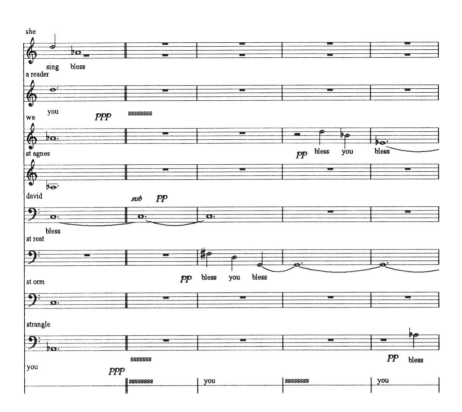

she

we con a- mor- e *ff* *mp*

a reader

e when i bless you bless sing bless sing bless

we *mp*

st agnes

david less me when i bless *ff* you bless *mp*

st reat less me when i bless - you bless *ff* *mp*

st orm

strangle

you bless you bless *p*

less less sssssss sssssss sssssss

very sssoftly

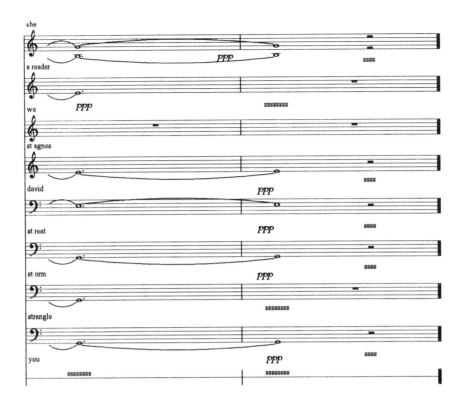

no path

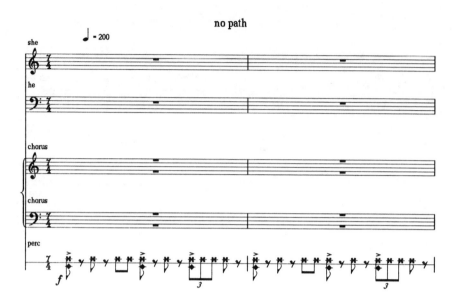

when the true path is ta- ken the way is clear tho the

when the true path is ta- ken the way is clear tho the

true path be not the near path and the price be dear no path but the true path should be ta- ken

true path be not the near path and the price be dear no path but the true path should be ta- ken

no   no road but the ho- ly road the   way   all o- ther roads

no   no road but the ho- ly road the   way   all o- ther roads

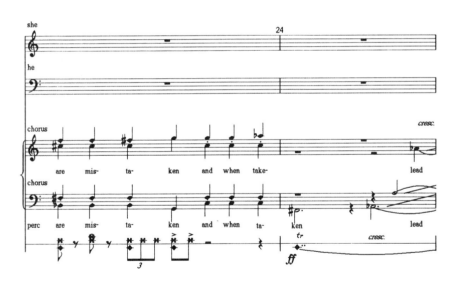

are mis- ta- ken and when take-   lead

are mis- ta- ken and when ta- ken   lead

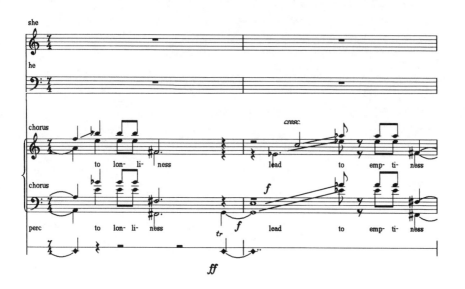

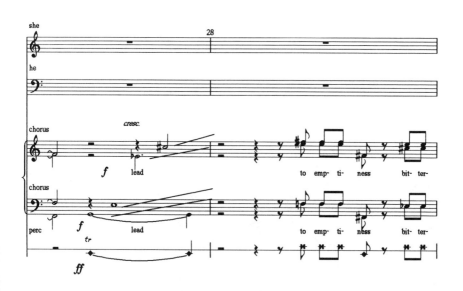

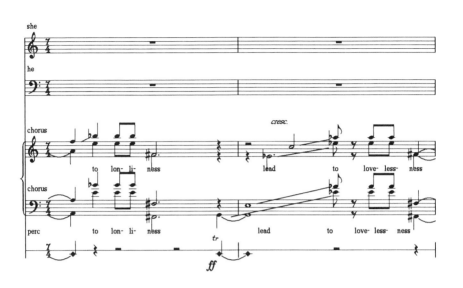

one and one

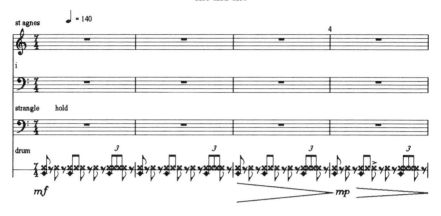

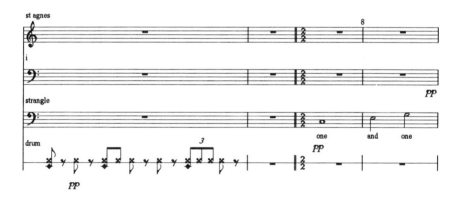

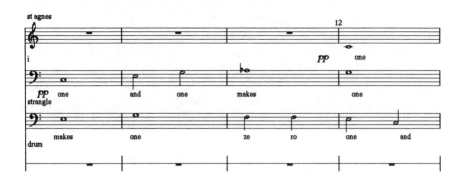

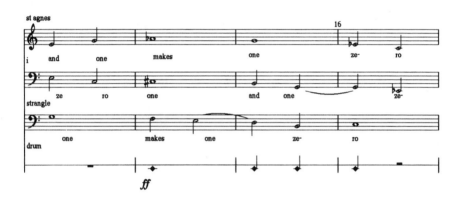

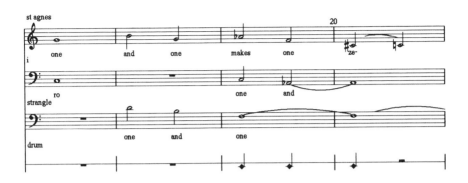

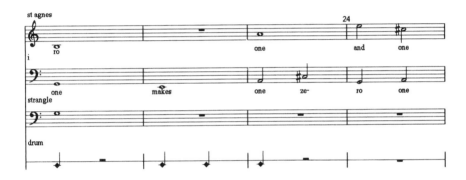

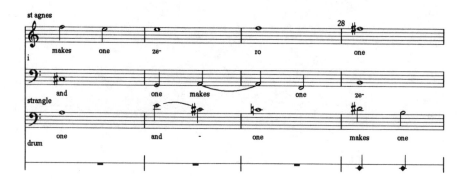

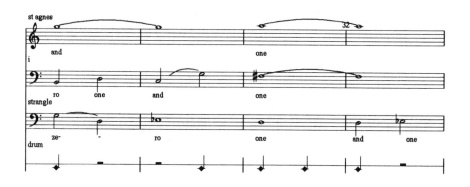

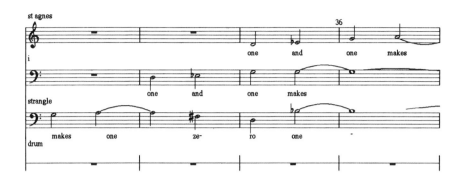

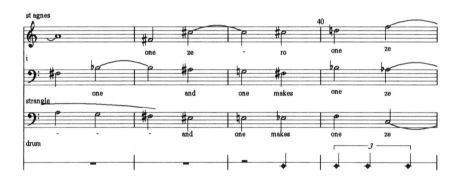

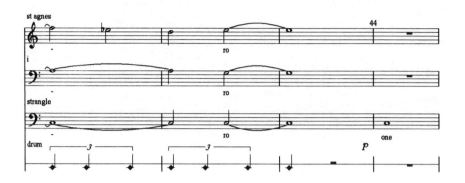

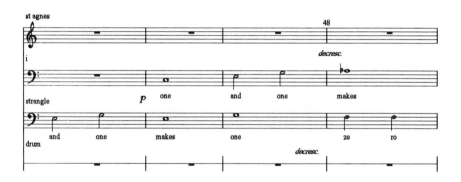

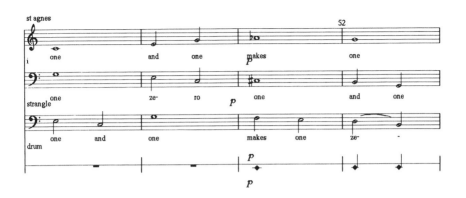

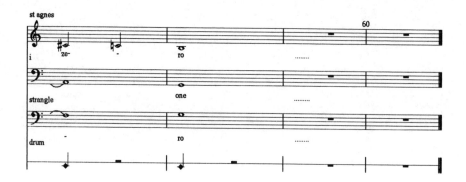

PRODUCTION NOTES
bpNichol

1) This piece is imagined as being performed in the kinds of halls & spaces choirs normally perform in. The performers' relationship to their audience should always remain that of itinerant chorus to moneyed audience.

2) In every performance there should be at least one person placed in the audience who will get up after "St. Reat's Song" and place some money in the hat and then go back to her/his seat.

3) The characters *never* call each other by name. Nor should their names be printed in any programme that accompanies the performance. Names exist as a guide to performers, and/or as part of the experience of reading the work, only.

4) The chorus should behave as a real chorus and leave space after each number for applause, acknowledging it if it comes. i should always be encouraged by any and all applause. It makes him even more ingratiating if there's a lot, and more depressed if there's a little.

5) Flags should be a variation on the following design:

The flags are always grouped in colour pairs i.e. black & red/red & black should be held by the same performer. The flags should always have black and at least one of the colour pairs should be red & black.

6) Performers get to keep all money they manage to collect from the audience by way of donation.

Editor for the Press: Christopher Dewdney
Typesetting: David McFadden
Printed in Canada

Coach House Press
50 Prince Arthur Ave., Suite 107
Toronto, Canada
M5R 1B5